My Real Life In Real Estate

My Real Life In Real Estate

By

RL Alexander

Conducting Creativity and Madu-Ndela Press

Copyright © 2022 by RL Alexander, Conducting Creativity in partnership with Madu-Ndela Press.

Cover credit: Jen Missouri.
Edited by: Conducting Creativity and Pen to Print Editing & Publishing

ISBN-13: 978-1-7368586-3-9

Contents

Acknowledgements	6
Author's Note	7
Preface	9
Introduction	12
The Act of Finishing	16
Who Am I and What Do I Want	19
Check Your Passion	26
Humble Beginnings	30
The Shortcomings	38
The Shift	42
Everyone Can't Drive The Boat	59
The Missing Piece of the Puzzle	63
The Uncommon Millionaire	67
Get Your Shit Together	68
Make Your Next Move Your Best Move	72
Synopsis	75
Appendix	77
Notes	88

Acknowledgements

To my spiritual advisor, God, I give you all the glory and praise for the wisdom that you have bestowed upon me through elders, life lessons, failures, successes, and overall journey. One thing I will mention when you are growing your empire is to have a hype man or woman in your corner. You need that person that will gas you up regardless of what the naysayers are spitting in your ear. For me, that person is my wife. Samantha, you push me and continue to encourage perfection in everything that I do. For that support and motivation, I love you unconditionally. Being your husband and a father to our children are my reasons to live. To my mom, sisters and family, you guys have always challenged me in different ways that I can apply back to my life. I am who I am today because of the guidance and love you have provided me with over the years. For that, I am eternally grateful.

Author's Note

This book was funded by the Alexander Transitional Housing Center (ATHC), a nonprofit created to train, house, and educate adolescents and adults starving for knowledge.

PREFACE

This book was written to serve as a beginner's guide to help motivate the competitive spirits who have become weary. For those who are worried about imminent failure rather than potential success. For those more worried about what could go wrong versus what could go right. This book is for you. Truth be told, you don't want every project or even your first one to go perfect, simply because you won't learn anything from perfection. Those who are successful know that the biggest and most memorable lessons come from mistakes and failures.

Don't let the hypothetical occurrences of what could happen stop you from making something happen.

My current success can be traced back to several mistakes and roadblocks I had to overcome early on in my career. Not only did I have to become better at discerning yield signs, but also have the grit to pick up the puzzle pieces along the way. Currently, I own thirty-two properties that consist of a four-unit apartment building, two duplexes, six single-family homes, ten new construction townhome duplexes that are under construction at this very moment, and nine single-family lots slated for construction in 2022. This book dives into the journey of my first flip, the people, the lessons, and the experiences that I had along the way.

On September 22, 2020, I started a nonprofit organization called the Alexander Transitional Housing Center (ATHC), which is currently under construction. Seeing this particular vision come to life has been quite an emotional journey for me. It is one of the many ways I've envisioned giving back to my hometown (Little Rock) and community. The ATHC works in collaboration with other local and nonlocal nonprofits, community members, entrepreneurs, and specialized industries and trainers to assist young adults, striving students, and up-and-coming community and world leaders via specialized training courses, perfect for on-the-grow learning. The nonprofit center (which will be duplicated around the world) will serve as a central hub where the local community can come and access the needed resources in that area. We offer job resources, skills training, adult education, entrepreneurship training and much more. In addition to a resource center for the community, ATHC also has a dormitory-style housing facility that houses select students between the ages of fifteen and eighteen, young adults between ages nineteen and twenty-five, and adults for a specified timeframe. Residents are put through training intensives that entail entrepreneurship training in an area of study that fits the student. Writing camps, artist retreats, culinary arts training, and more all at the expense of our community and corporate partners.

In the beginning of 2017, I owned two single-family properties and I thought I was doing big things for where I was in my real estate journey. It took a routinely scheduled Wednesday night at Elite Cigar Cafe based in Addison, TX to shift my perspective. The shift came on this particular night when my boy, we'll call him Mr. Worldwide, brought his cousin along. Sitting at a table, we discussed life, family, our nine-to-fives, side hustles, and businesses. Discussing our businesses, the cousin casually says he dabbles in real estate and I perked up immediately. Then and now, I have always been all ears when someone brought up real estate because I could apply every little nugget to my personal business. Mr. Worldwide's cousin continued to say that he owned over 120 properties with a mix of single-family homes and duplexes. My drive, enthusiasm, and love for the game of Monopoly made me realize that compared to the real estate portfolio he had accumulated, the two properties I owned weren't shit. This realization didn't upset me or make me feel less than, rather it was the motivation I needed to kick myself into the next gear.

Never let someone else's success make you feel like a failure but use it as fuel to drive your own success.

This was the turning point that made me realize that if real estate was something that I was really passionate about, I needed to focus more intently, make better decisions, and more calculated connections. Ever since, I have made a steadfast commitment to focus on growing my empire, putting in more work for myself than I would a job making someone else richer. I told myself that not working to obtain my dreams is worse than failing due to the fear of not getting started. If I stalled on taking actionable steps toward my goals because of distrusting myself, I would be consumed by a state of depression and left asking the infamous question: "What if?"

INTRODUCTION

The house is finally calm and there are sounds of thunderstorm winds coming from our sound machine next to our bed. My wife, son and daughter are in a deep sleep and it's peaceful knowing that they feel safe and comfortable while they dream. Suddenly my phone rings loudly, I immediately jump up to click the button on the side to silence the ring, because I can not afford the verbal lashing I would receive if I wake this 1 year old up and my wife has to get her.

I immediately run into my office, simultaneously answering the phone with a whisper, "Yes, hello this is Robert." My eyes are barely cracked open and I hear a voice on the other side in a panic yelling "Jefe! Wake up, wake up!" Immediately I recognize that it is Mario. "Yes, yes hermano, I am awake what's up?" At this point my stomach is in knots and my anxiety is on 10. "Jefe, these fucking people man! These fucking people!" says Mario. I can't understand what's wrong because he is not speaking in complete sentences but I can only assume that something has happened to him or my materials that I have on site. "Mario, I don't understand hermano. What's wrong?" Mario replies, "they stole it Jefe, they stole all of it!" I am pissed immediately because he can only be talking about my building materials. This is all too familiar and I have been here several times before but when he says all—I mean all of my shit is gone, what the fuck?! In a state of rage, I forget that everyone in the house is still sleeping including my in laws who live with us, after all it is only 6:30 in the morning.

I yell out, FUCK! Every time I try to do some good things for my community this is the thanks I get. Where are the police? Where are the neighbors? Where are the street politicians when you need them? I mean nobody saw shit? I am having a conversation with myself completely forgetting that Mario is on the phone and waiting for directions on what to do next. "Jefe, what do you want me to do?" asked Mario. "Give me a minute and I will call you back. I need to think!" Obviously I am in a state of rage and I can't provide him a clear answer now but it is also not his fault so I can't be upset with him. I take a beat. I settle my mind, have a bowl of cereal and I regroup. "Okay Robert, we need to call the police and file a report. We have insurance and that is what this is for. When the office opens up, call your bro and see of you are covered. It will be okay." I am back to talking to myself but this time I am not asking questions but offering solutions. Let's call Mario back. "Mario, go to Home Depot I am going to order more material to replace what was stolen and I will file a claim later. Right now I need to keep you and the guys working and I'll be in town first thing in the morning."

Damn what a morning and it's not even 8 o'clock yet, what else could go wrong? Oddly enough this is an easy problem to solve because all of the preparation protection parameters are in place for such a thing as this. I remember when I first got started in real estate everything was a penny pinch and having insurance was a cost I didn't think I could afford. You would sort of hope and pray nothing went wrong or got stolen. But now 10 years in the game and 2 years in on new construction you learn that a gamble like that doesn't make sense and is damn sure not good for business. I live in Texas and my developments and overall company is based out of my home state, Arkansas. Dealing with logistics and coordination is a big part of my job. Almost just as much as doing the physical work which I also do. I now have to pack and prepare to drive to Little Rock so that I can lay my eyes on everything and directly deal with this morning's setback.

Next morning I am up early and on the road by 3 am because I have always enjoyed rising early and driving into the sun. My black-on-black 2017 Sierra Denali truck's motor has the calmest sound: I welcome it in the mornings. This morning, the hum is almost melodic; not too loud- steady and moving; just like me. See, I live in the world of real estate and construction and something is always happening. As I make into town I ride past my first property that I ever renovated. It offers me a feeling of nostalgia every time I see it. It reminds me of where I started and provides a humbling timeline for where I am now. As I turn the corner to my latest project, both of my cell phones are ringing. In the passenger seat are proposals and plans for my next big development which I am presenting in a few hours. Rounding the corner I see all that is right, a busy construction crew, Mexican music playing loudly over a handheld speaker, the sound of framing nails, hammering and saw blades creating a wonderful orchestra. However, as I get closer, I see all that is wrong. I answer my business cell quickly telling them to hold as I answer my spouse on my personal cell (allowing my wife and family to be second is not an option). Hanging up from her call, I tell the business caller, I will meet you in thirty minutes.

Barely throwing the gear in park, I swing out of my truck, changing into my work boots, motor still running, and door left open, I yell and whistle to Mario, "Wrong spot hermano"! Turning around to the trackhoe operator; I hand signal to turn off the machine so that they can hear me speak. The crew quickly gathers around. I reach in my truck for some donuts and energy drinks which I hope will add balance to my message. This dirt is now my conference room, this team is building my dream. I take out my Spanish for Construction quick guide and begin to explain the mistakes as well as the direction for the day. I am still learning Spanish so I miss a few things but the message is understood. Also, Mario speaks English as well and as their boss he can make up for any of the messaging I lack. Now I am ready to get to work because I honestly enjoy this part of my business. This is where my passion and my enjoyment really thrive, out here on the grid iron. See being the boss is great. Being the one to write checks, make the important decisions, having meetings and building relationships all have their purpose. But you have to create a balance. A balance where the people you work with and that work for you know that you are not just the one writing checks but you are the one who will out work them if need be. You know your stuff just like they do. You have to be well rounded and for me that means getting your hands dirty.

In my field, I am a subject matter expert - not because of my tenure in this game, but because of my work and my knowledge. I can tell you not only what I know but what I actually do. Currently, I am building 25 brand new homes, I own 7 rental properties with a mix of single family and multi-family and I do it all while remaining a good husband, an amazing father, dependable son and a great friend. As I sit here writing this, I think back to where it all began and where to start my story? I can only conclude that it should start just like a house and I should began with my foundation. So this is Robert and this is "My Real Life in Real Estate!"

Chapter One

THE ACT OF FINISHING

So you thought that this would be okay? You thought that I would just lay down and accept this from you? You can't honestly think that I'd be cool with you taking my money, giving me a little excitement, and bouncing. I thought we meant more to each other than that. But I see. When times get hard and the world says how we used to feel about each other is no longer correct, you just go on to the highest bidder. Where is your loyalty? Oh, I get it. I was just a transaction in this relationship, and I only mean as much to you as our last intimate moment. But I poured everything into you! My time and my attention, even when others demanded more of it. I gave it to you. I gave you my love, tears, and money. So much money! All you care about is the transaction. So I guess this is where we are. You were my foundation and I was only your guest. Damn! I celebrated in your highs and cried in your lows, but through it all we continued to build together. Our past has been shaky, but we can renovate our future. I may never have your complete loyalty, however, I love it. I love you. From the first time I met you, touched you, smelled you, learned your history, shared my past… I knew that I was in love…

Prior to writing this book about my journey into real estate investing, I pondered what angle to take. I thought about great stories written by successful women and men outlining the "x" key points you need to know about real estate in order to succeed. The books are always labeled something like this: "The Three Things You Need to Know to Become a Millionaire in Real Estate"; "Ten Big Things You Could Be Doing Right Now That Would Change Your Life in Real Estate"; "The Number One Move That Separates You From Your Competitors in Real Estate." I've read many of these books, and granted, some hold certain truths, but the reality is there is not a certain number of steps that you can take that will guarantee your success in real estate. In fact, the one thing you can do is try, fail, and try again. That is the only thing that breeds success.

When I think about real estate investing, attending college comes to mind. If you can make a commitment to complete college, **the act of finishing** will breed confirmation in you that says, "I can achieve anything I put my mind to." This is not to say that college and real estate are one in the same, but that both have trials and rewards. However, there are some key differences. If you think that you can read a few books, talk to a few people, and then BOOM, go buy a property and make a million dollars, you are sadly mistaken. Don't get me wrong. Has it happened before? Absolutely, the lottery has been hit by one hit wonders! But just because you pick five random numbers and win big, that doesn't make you a genius, it makes you lucky. *And though I wish that luck on all of us, with real estate, it takes time, it takes drive, it takes initiative, and most importantly, it takes the will to know that no matter how many times you fail, it is not a failure, but a lesson on what not to do the next time.* And you keep going.

Chapter One: Time to Reflect

- ◊ Is there a time or was there a time where you felt like quitting?

- ◊ What did you do?

- ◊ Describe a time when you wanted to quit but you pushed through.

- ◊ What feeling did you have after you completed the task?

- ◊ What can you ask and tell yourself in the future when the idea of quitting something you want to do resurfaces?

Chapter Two:

WHO AM I AND WHAT DO I WANT

My interest in real estate stemmed from the curiosity of how the one percent were making their money. How does the average earner become well-off, the well-off become rich, and the rich become wealthy? Real estate! Now, this is not the only thing. Sure, you have your Zuckerbergs, fintech guys, stock market investors, business owners, and so on. However, somewhere in their portfolio, they have real estate.

So here we are, my freshman year of college. Initially, I was one hundred percent sure that I wanted to be a dentist like my uncle. After graduating from dental school, I was going to practice beside him for several years, take over his practice while he worked reduced hours, and then reach back to high school classmates and college friends to grow the book of business. I would be set for life. Freshman year, I took my prerequisites and for my major I selected biology with an emphasis in pre-dental. Easiest decision I had to make.

Freshman year was a blast and a blur. With all the structure and steadfastness that I had in high school, classes were easy for me. I now had all this time and days to complete my work versus high school where it was due by the next day or day after next. With that mindset, freshman year was simple to me. Many incoming students are expected to mess up their first year and a half, maybe even two, but if you do well your first year, you are somewhat ahead of the curve. I spent that year getting acclimated to college life and going to classes, while also being an adult learning how to manage time, responsibilities, and partying. My first year was critical for me because it set the tone for what was to come. In my freshman year, I saw thugs enroll in school (while still gangbanging), get tuition overpayment checks, use it to buy a bubble caprice, sit it on twenty-two inch rims, put in a sound system, a couple bricks of marijuana, and then drop out of school as if they just received a sign-on bonus to the league. Crazy!

I experienced partying from Thursday until Sunday with classes bright and early Monday morning. I witnessed girls taking showers in the boys bathrooms. I saw Greeks for the first time, which blew my mind. There I was, a kid from a somewhat small city, experiencing all of those new things by myself for the first time. It was everything I expected and wanted college to be. Well, before I knew about Historically Black Colleges and Universities (HBCUs). And icing on the cake, I signed up for my first major credit card so I could get a free Subway footlong. This was not only a critical moment in my life concerning financial responsibilities and my credit journey, but also a moment to reflect on why I applied for the credit card in the first place. My story isn't unique in this way since countless other college students applied for credit cards because food was promised. So, like I said, freshman year was a blast and a blur.

Beginning of sophomore year, I was still committed to my biology major and becoming a dentist; but, I had made another commitment. During summer, a friend and I decided to give Greek life a chance. We started the pledging process to become members of Kappa Alpha Psi Fraternity, Inc. Summer was easy for me—not many distractions to knock me off course. However, when fall semester started, classes became a little more intense. Not to forget, I was pledging at the same time. Fall semester was okay with classes, but the spring semester was an absolute disaster. I was only averaging four hours of sleep per night plus the ten to twenty minute naps that I may have gotten throughout the day. My GPA began to take a dip and those biology lab classes started to kick my ass, but I was committed to finishing the process. I don't want to gloss over the subject and make it seem as though pledging was easy and the worst was just a lack of sleep. In fact, I think the easiest thing was not sleeping. But it's hardwired in me that once I start something, I have to finish and see it through no matter how hard or tough the challenge may be. The opportunity to pledge a Black fraternity with all of its historical significance and rituals made me a stronger and more focused individual. I owned the distractions that it caused and accepted the consequences—good and bad. I appreciate all the lessons that the process taught me. In Spring 2007, I became a Nupe. I crossed my line as the five club out of seven line brothers, and we were set to act a fool—at least for the next semester. The foolishness caught up soon enough.

By the end of sophomore year, not only was I a couple of classes behind in my degree, but my GPA was low as hell. Spring semester, my focus shifted to making some money because my swag had to match my affiliation, or so I thought. My job became my top priority, Greek life second, and school was third. I went from a 3.8 GPA and dean's list during freshman year to a 2.9 GPA and ready to change my major. Dental school wasn't looking so hot, but I made a commitment to finish my undergraduate program.

Summer 2007 called for self-reflection. I realized I was a full semester behind in school and needed to figure some shit out quickly. I decided to work all summer and save some money so that I didn't have to work during my junior year. I got a job working at a clothing retailer in the mall. During this time, I got my second credit card. By the end of summer, I saved enough money to support myself through the semester and shifted my focus back to school.

During the fall semester of junior year, I was very focused, but somewhere along the way I decided to change my major a bit because I realized I didn't have the passion—there is that word again—to be a dentist. I was chasing money versus purpose. I shifted my major to biology with a focus in health sciences. Slightly easier, but still accomplished the goal of graduating with a degree in biology like I planned originally. The first semester was somewhat successful. I was still active with the frat, serving as treasurer for the past year and a half. Through a friend I was able to get a job working as a Financial Service Representative (FSR), a fancy name for a Bank Teller. Then, another major turning point happened . . . .

I started working at a local bank as a FSR and saw a new side to the cash game. Of course there is the simple side: you get a job, open an account, get a debit card, make a deposit, and withdraw funds when needed. Whether you manage it well or not, you become a part of the banking industry. However, I was on the inside of the banking industry and witnessed with my own eyes how they made money. I saw how the rich continued to get richer and the poor struggled to hold on. I observed and learned how someone who spent ten dollars on groceries with only five dollars in their account would be charged thirty-five dollars in non-sufficient funds fees (NSF). Now they not only owed the bank the five dollars they didn't have, but also an additional thirty-five dollars in fees. Before they got their next check, they were already in the hole. Now, don't get me wrong, rich people have money issues as well and they are a lot larger than five dollars, but the difference is they will turn around and deposit ten thousand dollars versus someone's $450 payroll check. The difference is they know Tom who is the bank manager and best friend to the vice president. Tom will not only reverse those NSF charges, but he will also lend them credit until they can make their deposit in thirty days. See, the biggest thing that was reiterated in banking was the main thing I learned from my mom and every other Black adult. The saying goes, "It's not what you know but who you know!" Funny thing is, they applied that to whatever situation they were in. If it was a church, then "who you know" is God! If it was at work, then "who you know" was the boss. If it was at a Greek party, then "who you know" was your best friend's boyfriend who was working the door! I quickly learned the same rule applied at the bank. And then some.

    As I got older, I understood that, yes, in some cases who I knew would get me certain places, but in most instances, I also needed to know something about what I was doing. Who you know will only get you so far if you don't know enough about what you're doing. A potential connection could soon become a burnt bridge if proper preparation wasn't taken (e.g., education, application of knowledge, skills). On the other hand, being ready for that big shot can also open doors to the most important conversation after "Who do you know?" and "What do you know?": "Who knows you?"

    During my time at the bank, I did what I do best. I am an extrovert by character and I uphold myself to high standards of dignity, honesty, humbleness, and respect. I made sure everyone that I encountered experienced that. I am also an inquisitive person who doesn't mind asking questions. I became good associates with my manager, the branch manager, and loan officers. I worked extra shifts not only because I could use the money, but also to show them that I was willing to go the extra mile. If someone called in, I took it. They started noticing how dependable I was. FSRs were compensated extra by selling bank credit cards and I pushed myself to stay number one in the region. The intentionality I had about my personal growth at the bank created a turning point in my life because that branch, along with a specific loan officer, gave me my first opportunity in real estate.

Jim was a great guy. He never looked at my age unless it was to compliment me on how wise I was for my age. He never looked at my race, prejudged my intelligence level, or shunned me when I would run into his office and talk about finances. Jim would take the time to listen, provide life wisdom, and feedback on every topic we discussed. He was definitely a mentor for me and taught me a great deal over a pivotal two-year span in my life. Reflecting on this very moment while I write this book, I can only think about how this time assisted me and my career. It was not only who I knew, but also what I had learned and who knew who I was due to my work ethic at the bank that warranted me worthy of opportunities to venture into doors I had yet imagined existed.

So, I knew hands down who I was, but the question was, "What did I want?" And to go a step further, "How was I going to get what I wanted?" I knew I wanted a life of financial security and freedom and I was willing to play the game to get it. I landed the job at the bank my junior year and created a stable source of income for my remaining two years in college.

In answering the question of what I wanted, I had begun mapping out the details on how to accomplish my goals. I acknowledged that the road ahead was long, rough and rugged, but through persistence and determination, I would get there eventually. Pledging helped to shape some of my ambitions and determination because of everything I had to go through to come out on the other side. Pledging had a hands-on way of showing me that everything else is easy compared to the random phone calls, chores, and late nights I went through during my process.

By my senior year of college, I had been at the bank for two years and I had met some very interesting and influential people. In fact, my first career job post college came from a business owner who also worked as a director for a technology company in which I was a sales representative. I mean, how completely left could you go considering I started off wanting to be a dentist?! Reflecting, I now understand that all my steps, strolls, plummetting GPA, refocusing, late nights, and early mornings were all a part of the divine plan that I didn't see but later realized. I mean, who would've thought my 2.8 GPA during sophomore year aligned with my ten-year goal of becoming financially free? I couldn't fathom at that moment that a ham and turkey footlong would propel me to an 850 credit score. I was just hungry. But along this journey, my passion grew. I discovered what real hunger was.

So to recap, this biology major who would've bet his high school allowance on becoming a dentist, realized gunk, tar, and built-up plaque wasn't his passion. So, I regrouped, shifted, and refocused to create a better plan.

Chapter Two: Time to Reflect

- ◊ Think back to those earlier moments in your life (they don't have to be childhood, but they can be) when you were figuring yourself out. What was a defining moment that created a turning point?

- ◊ Thinking about the title of this chapter, do you know who you are and what it is that you want? Who is it and where are they going in life?

- ◊ Have you created or written down a plan to accomplish what it is that you want? If not, start now.

- ◊ Did you ever have something that derailed you from your plans? How did you get back on track?

- ◊ Obstacles can beome challenges. How will you overcome those challenges?

Chapter Three

CHECK YOUR PASSION

In the beginning, I started to ease into real estate by completing handyman jobs. Clients would ask me to do jobs like installing ceiling fans or running a new outlet for them to mount their TV higher. I looked at these jobs as a way to check my passion. I wanted to ensure that this was something that I enjoyed doing and that my drive would reflect my work. What does that mean? If I am adamant about a job, then my completed work should show that I gave it one hundred percent effort.

Now that we've gotten the fluff shit out of the way, let's have a real conversation. How did a Black man whose background fits the stereotypical Black family (i.e., raised by a single parent with no husband or father presence in the household, low- to middle income, food stamps, free or reduced school lunch plan, star athlete, and possibly a recipient of federal aid for college) accomplish what I've accomplished? Better yet, why does this same Black man think that he can get a loan from my bank and I can't even qualify my own people? Yeah, that's how it started. So what makes me different? The same things that made me highly qualified also made me a threat and questionable.

In the movie *ATL*, which I think is a great movie by the way, Jackie Long plays a character by the name of Esquire. Esquire is best friends with the main character, Rashad, lives on the same side of the hood as him, and even enjoys some of the same extracurriculars as Rashad. The difference? Esquire attends a prep school on the opposite side of town. Esquire is trying to obtain admission to an Ivy League School, but realizes that even though he meets all the requirements and in some cases exceeds them, he still needs a letter of recommendation from someone of high stature to better his chances of acceptance at the school. To take it a step further, the only person he may know is a Black man that plays golf at the clubhouse in which he caddies for. After reaching out to this potential sponsor, Mr. Garnett makes him go through hell and high water just to get a letter that he should have volunteered to write after getting to know Esquire. Mr. Garnett eventually writes the letter, which is a happy ending, but there are underlying issues that need to be addressed such as: Why is it that a Black man has to work twice as hard for something that he is overqualified to receive? Why is it that when certain Black people become successful, they remove the ladder as opposed to lifting as we climb? Better yet, I would prefer we make it and immediately turn around to bring up the next man. And how do we begin bridging the gaps that exist in our own communities? Oftentimes, we seem to want to make it even harder for those that come after us! When I thought about what I wanted to put in this book, I realized I wanted to briefly tell my story, both failures and successes. I wanted to make it as real as possible with none of the extra fluff that is unnecessary and used to fill space. I prefer talking to people and helping them one-on-one, however a book, this book, can reach the masses. It is my aim to answer some of the questions that I receive on a consistent basis around how to get started in real estate and what I did early on to create the success that I am now experiencing. Keep in mind, these are my steps, my failures, and my successes. This is not a manual to be considered as absolute. However, these are standard things that you will experience along your journey.

> *"I told him, "Please don't die over the neighborhood*
> *That your mama rentin'*
> *Take your drug money and buy the neighborhood*
> *That's how you rinse it." -* Jay Z

I like this line and several others in the song, *Story of OJ* by Jay Z. This line in particular because Jay talks about drug dealers and how they can evolve from the simple life of crime and basically do what most successful people do now. Take your flip money and put it into a sustainable model with less legal risk. Using the lyrics from this song to make an example, let's look at it this way: Drug dealers take risks every day when selling. They risk their life dealing with other drug dealers wanting to take their block. They risk their freedom ducking and dodging 12 (the police), who want to lock them up for life for committing a crime that is considered to be against the law, mainly because they're not paying taxes on that income. They risk their re-up money (funds used to purchase more dope) hoping that the next drop will allow them to make the same amount of money or more as the last drop. However, imagine if they repurposed that risk into buying the same neighborhood that they're tearing down and building it up for better, exchanging their risk of life and freedom for a life of financial freedom. I tried the method of the drug dealer once but quickly realized that wasn't the life I wanted. The fear of my life being taken by death or incarceration didn't satisfy the risk for me. I found something better for my life. Something where my past wouldn't haunt my future.

"What's more important than throwing money in a strip club? Credit." -Jay Z

We are taught at a very early age how to be nice, have manners, eat with our mouths closed, say "Please" and "Thank you," and all of the things we think will make us perfect ladies and gentlemen in the world. However, what we fail to do is teach our children and family about financial responsibility. Most of the time it is due to the fact that we don't have financial control ourselves.

A credit score of 850 is a perfect credit score and is viewed by creditors as someone who has a good grasp on controlling their finances, is financially responsible, and low risk for a creditor. **I have an 850 credit score**. I have multiple trade lines on my credit report. I have owned, sold, and retained plenty of homes, and my goal now is to reach back to help build my community—my people. My aim is to be a reference guide to help assist you when you get stuck, a mirror when you need to reflect, and most importantly, a reminder that what you are going through is nothing new. Although the experience may be foreign to you, there is nothing new under the sun, therefore, don't quit—especially in your financial journey. And last but not least: **Having good credit is not just for the rich.**

Chapter Three: Time to Reflect

- ◊ Now that you know who you are, what is it that you are passionate about?

- ◊ Many of us make decisions for a plethora of reasons when it comes to what it is that we want to do in/with our lives. What are your reasons and do they align with your passion?

- ◊ Deep Thought- Which one is more important to you: having a great credit score, or having a bunch of money in the bank? (Hint: They are equally as important but what are your thoughts?)

- ◊ Do you think it is worth your time and energy to work at a job or start a business that you are not passionate about?

Chapter Four

HUMBLE BEGINNINGS

"As kids, we didn't complain about being poor; we talked about how rich we were going to be and made moves to get the lifestyle we aspired to by any means we could. And as soon as we had a little money, we were eager to show it." - Jay Z

Like many others, having good credit wasn't something that I was taught, nor was it top of mind. Although the term "credit" wasn't used, the principles of reputation and trustworthiness were instilled. At thirteen I was borrowing video games from friends, exchanging shoes with my cousins, borrowing a lawnmower because I had started my own lawn service business, and a host of other things. Because I returned the items I borrowed in its proper condition, this bettered my reputation. Borrowing something from someone comes with liability and a responsibility to make sure it is returned in the same condition or better than when it was given. This same principle that I was taught at thirteen can be applied to financial education and building good credit.

A credit card is an entity that has let you borrow something which must be returned in the same condition or better. This entity has let you borrow cash in the form of credit and you are responsible for returning that credit in the form of cash in the same amount in which it was given or better. "Better" in this instance is considered interest. Being a good steward of what was given, taking care of it, and returning it in the same condition or better not only makes you a better person, but also will guide you on the path to building good credit.

It is honestly that simple. A credit card doesn't care if you are male or female, Black or white, young or old. It simply wants to be treated with respect, responsibility, and paid back in full in a timely manner. If you want to grow credit, get a credit card, use it, and pay it back. That's the formula!

The habits we created from youth have an impact on our financial responsibilities as adults. When I borrowed a video game with the intent of playing it for a certain period of time, I knew that I had to give it back because it was not my game to keep. I had to make sure that I returned the game in a timely manner and in the condition that it was given, or I was responsible, here is that word again, for replacing that game. Since I created that habit earlier, it was very easy for me to transition to larger deals and larger payments when I got older. At the same time, I had friends and family who I had to call and remind to return my belongings. I had to scold them most times because things they borrowed weren't returned in the same state as when I gave it to them. I also had to remind them that they were responsible for the material that they asked me to borrow. Personal respect was lost due to property disrespect, disregard, and distrust. Keeping in stride with the beginning of this book, imagine if the drug dealer didn't pay the plug—the person that has the drugs for them to buy—the money owed to them. What would happen to the drug dealer? Consequences could be detrimental.

Being irresponsible can lead to negative habits being created. The people mentioned above are the ones who are continually being called by creditors for them to pay their bill when a credit card payment is due. Auto companies have to remind them that their payment is past due, and the utility companies are threatening to shut off services. You are the one who asked them for credit! You are the one who took the auto loan! You are the one who has to be responsible to pay it back! Now, don't get me wrong, there are some instances in which children who didn't have anything to do with their credit score or journey have bad credit because their mother or father received a credit card in their name and proceeded to perform the same bad habits in their child's name that they did in their own name. There's nothing you can do as a child about this but once you are an adult, you can start your path to recovering your credit through different programs such as fraud assistance and simply by being a good steward of your own credit card once you get one.

"True to my oath, they proud of my growth. I come from the turf, I doubled my worth." -Nipsey Hussle

Respect, responsibility, integrity, humility, humbleness, and wisdom are some of the basic principles that were instilled in me from my mother, my siblings, and other adults in my life. Because I'm a developer whose sole responsibility is cultivating the grounds from concept to fruition, I will make a lot of references to building. Homes must have a good, solid foundation. Without a solid foundation, the home you build on top of it will crumble. Visualize a concrete slab foundation that is weak and has cracks. Picture still deciding to build the house. The house that is built adds weight, weight that the poorly poured foundation can't withstand. Now, imagine the house is all built. You start to notice cracks in the wall, nothing is straight, and water leaks through the roof when it rains. Finally, you realize you wasted all of that time and money **because the foundation wasn't solid.** The concept of building a solid foundation was no different for me in my humble beginnings. My mother made sure to instill a firm bedrock on which my dreams and goals would one day manifest themselves. Many times as people, we fail to instill these basic principles in our children mainly because somewhere along the way we have abandoned the principles ourselves. Respect should be a part of that foundational principle that allows us to see another individual for exactly that, an individual. Regardless of race, creed, or color, each of us are unique in our own way, and until we learn to respect our own and others' individuality and not marginalize people because they don't fit our institutionalized ways of thinking, we can't grow. I had a difficult time becoming who I was meant to be because I was constantly trying to live up to the standards put on me versus blooming from the seed that God had put inside of me. Meanwhile, the judgemental person struggles with stagnant growth due to being lost in somebody else's vision, ultimately blinding their own.

Respect is taught from the basic principles of having respect for elders. But what if their perspective is limited? What if they are stuck in their ways? What if their advice stems from a time period when milk was five cents, and now it's fifteen dollars? Am I disrespecting them because I don't believe that their way is absolute? Am I not showing respect because I choose to live a different life than the way they lived theirs? Absolutely not! Times have changed, the world is different, thus my perspective has evolved. On my end and as a voice for a younger generation, respect is acknowledging and listening to the wisdom of our elders and not forsaking the validity in their messages. Tupac said it best when he rapped, "What more can I say? I wouldn't be here today if the old skool didn't pave the way." On the contrary, it is my desire that the older generations aim to understand who I am, who we are, and who we evolve to be. Condemning me for my choices simply pushes me away, but providing warnings on mistakes and roadtraps ahead with gentle, patient, yet firm direction is more likely to be received.

The next two go together for me: responsibility and integrity. Growing up, I had chores that had to be completed before being able to do something that I wanted to do. It could have been as simple as sleeping over a relative's house, but I knew that I had to complete those chores before I could do anything! One chore in particular was cleaning my room. That involved making my bed, putting away my dirty clothes, folding my clean clothes, and vacuuming my bedroom floor. Other things were a part of my chores but for the sake of the story and example, I will keep it simple: cleaning "my" room was "my" responsibility. On this particular Friday, I wanted to spend the weekend over at a relative's house. My room was on the top of my list of chores. I made my bed, no problem. I put my dirty clothes in the hamper, no problem, and I even vacuumed spick and span. The problem came when I had to fold my clean clothes and put them away either by hanger or putting them in the drawer. On this day, I was ready to go and I decided that all my clean clothes were dirty and I would put them in the dirty clothes hamper. After doing this I told my mom that all my chores were completed and that I was ready to go. She completed a quick once over and dropped me off at my cousins' house.

After a few hours of kicking it like we did back in the day, my aunt came into the room and killed the vibe with one sentence. "Robert, your mom is on her way to come get you and take you home." I'm confused and wondering if something happened. Did I leave something at home she needs me to get? We still had 007 to play and jokes to laugh at, and we hadn't even gotten to the pizza! This was strange. So, my mom gets there, tells me to get all of my things because, "You are not coming back this weekend," and we begin to head home. All I can think of is something went wrong with someone in the family and we have to go see them. We get home and I go up to my room and see all of those clothes that were clean that I threw in the hamper. They stared at me from my bed and I knew that fresh switches or a leather belt to my ass was soon to follow. "Oh shit!" runs through my head, and if I wasn't already scared I would have said it aloud. I almost crapped my pants. I'm caught, and not only did I lose my chance of spending the weekend with my cousins, I am about to get a grade A ass whooping for lying, let alone the punishment that would follow.

Now, that is an early life story example, but one that may be more relevant today is that as a developer, I have accounts with several vendors—lumber companies, appliance companies, and even sub-contractors. I have an account with them and my responsibility is to pay them back within thirty days of when I receive a statement for items purchased. I must have the integrity that I will honor my word and responsibilities to make those payments, and on the off chance that something happens where I can't pay in full or on time, I am completely honest about it and tell them when I can pay. The moral of the story is, I had a responsibility and due to my lack of integrity, I failed to complete my chores adequately, and it cost me. Same thing with my vendors. If I don't pay them, I can lose my account access with them. That means no more credit terms, but instead everything has to be paid in full up front.

Now, let's refocus on this small lie (dirty clothes) and the overall view. Little white lies lead to bigger, more mischievous lies. What once would only cost an ass whooping and loss of family visitation for the weekend now can cost serious financial burden, loss of property, credit score, jobs, friends and family, and maybe even jail time. The problems may have started because our foundational principles weren't established and set in place, **but it is never too late.**

"It's never too late and you're never too old to become better!" ~ Anonymous

The next two principles also go together: humility and humbleness. The story above taught me an early lesson on humility. At age thirteen, how does it look to my cousins, that close to midnight, when I should be staying up late and having fun, I'm packing up my clothes to go home and never return? How does it look when I'm asked, "Cuz, what happened to you?" Either I have to tell the truth by admitting I lied to my mom about folding clothes or lie to my cousin about lying (and the cycle continues). Keep in mind, I'm walking funny because I got whooped for the lie as well. I am one hundred percent embarrassed and more than ashamed at this point. I can't keep letting this happen, so what are my realistic options? I can receive humility and then learn to be humble for the responsibilities and opportunities I'm given. I can learn to be a good steward over the small things I am given and understand that bigger and better opportunities will be given to me in the future. Most importantly, I can learn the principle of wisdom. Wisdom comes from knowing, listening, understanding, and growth. One of my favorite prayers or at least a passage is from the serenity prayer. The prayer goes like this, "God grant me the serenity to accept the things I cannot change; the courage to change the things I can; and the wisdom to know the difference!" No, I was never in AA or anything like that and one could argue that the verse is less about wisdom and more about the acceptance of human weakness and surrendering your fate to that of a higher power—amor fati. However, the way I see it is that knowledge comes from the growth of going through life's trials and tribulations, but wisdom comes when you learn from other's trials and tribulations. If I see you run into a brick wall, hit your head, and start bleeding, I don't have to do the same thing in order to know that it will hurt and that I shouldn't do it myself. ***I was faced with a choice to make.***

Life is a constant battle of knowledge and wisdom. We may have to go through things first and gain knowledge to give to someone else after us, but we should always be passing information down. When we pass it down, we have to know that it is our responsibility to do it with respect and integrity. When we receive wisdom, we must understand the person is giving it to us with humility, which we must humbly accept and continue to pass on. One could argue that wisdom can't be received from another. Knowledge can be received, but wisdom comes from marrying experience with that knowledge. I would say, whatever your beliefs are for how you obtain knowledge or gain wisdom, use it. There is not and never will be one way that fits all people. We must find what works for us and use that. Our foundation is what sets our life on its course to have dreams, establish goals, and understand our shortcomings. How we choose to deal with the many and ever-changing shifts that will continue to happen throughout our lives is a part of the journey. Therefore, when you look at yourself and think about where you are currently, evaluate your foundation and what your life is built upon. Is your life built on respect? Is it built on lies and deceit? What is your G-code? Regardless, know that if your foundation is cracked, rocky, has shifted a little, or if you have no foundation at all, it is never too late to start over and build solidly. After all, a house with a good foundation can last for generations and that is what you are working to build. Legacy.

"Where your backbone, n*, where your code at?" -Nipsey Hussle

Chapter Four: Time to Reflect

- ◊ How would you describe your humble beginnings?

- ◊ What foundational qualities were instilled in you from your childhood (or maybe even adolescene years)?

- ◊ What habits have you tried to break and what habits have you tried to create in order to improve your life?

- ◊ Thinking back through the chapter, what key take aways can you apply to your life and foundational principles?

- ◊ How does intergrity play a role in your everyday actions?

- ◊ Do you feel like you can be taught and improve or are you stuck in your own ways? How can you change your mentality?

Chapter Five

THE SHORTCOMINGS

What are shortcomings? A better question is: How do you define shortcomings? I have shortcomings everyday. My job thinks I can be doing more. I don't get everything done on my Honey-Do list that my wife likes to create for me everyday. I could probably call my family and friends more. My son who is three and full of energy wants me to play with him more, but life sometimes gets in the way. I have shortcomings daily. The dictionary defines shortcomings as a fault or failure to meet a certain standard, typically in a person's character, a plan, or a system. So, let's unbox this definition because the language used here, and its meaning can be broad. If your shortcomings can be defined by a system, who or what defines the system? Don't overthink the question, but think about what I'm asking you. If the system is what defines a shortcoming and you don't constantly adhere to the rules or "status quo" of the system, then you by definition will always have shortcomings. Understanding this is powerful. If you know that you will always have shortcomings due to the system that you are comparing yourself to, then you should go after your goals without the concern of playing to the system. In fact, create your own system.

> *"You know, we all feel like the system is too big to change, but guess what? We are the system, and we need to change."* - Dr. Max Goodwin, New Amsterdam (TV series)

I would say that I created my system from experiences, trial and error, knowledge, faith, and at times luck. I experienced a lot growing up where my mom had expectations of who I should be and what I should do. I had my own expectations of and for myself, and I coupled those with milestones that I tried to accomplish that didn't work out as planned. I learned to shift. A lot of reading, which provided some level of knowledge, helped to shape my mind around the world's definition of success and failure. And then you have good ol' fashion luck that provides that unexpected boost during times of need. Another great thing about developing your own system is that you can shift at any given moment and it is completely your choice.

After graduating from high school and starting college, I knew beyond a shadow of doubt that I was going to school to become a dentist like my uncle. I had a full plan already mapped out. I would enroll in school and choose my major the very first semester. No need to explore, wait, and see. No, I needed to sign up for all of my biology, chemistry, and anatomy classes because I needed those courses in order to get into dental school. After I passed my undergraduate curriculum I would get into dental school on the first shot, no issues. By the way, I was planning to graduate college in 3.5 years versus the normal four to five years that everyone else does. After I got into dental school, I would graduate from there in four years and I would work under my uncle for an additional four to five years or until he felt like retiring and leaving me his entire book of business. The vision was clear and I had it completely mapped out. "But God," as Granny would say, "had other plans, baby."

It's funny how we think we can use Siri and GPS in our lives. Oftentimes, we don't account for the love, unexpected love, as well as tragedy, and devastation. The unpredictable, coupled with your ability to receive and grow, will likely alter, if not even just a little, your vision. My initial vision obviously didn't happen in the way I had planned. You'd be reading a different love story if it did.

I looked at my inability to accomplish my goal of going to dental school as a shortcoming when in fact it was only a shift and refocus. For me, this is where spirituality comes into play because I feel that all things happen for a reason—good and bad—even though we rarely like to accept the bad.

I went to school and took a year—as advised by my freshman counselor—

to choose a major. My second year of school I pledged a fraternity. By junior year, I was already a semester behind due to foolishness from the previous semester; I started working because I needed spending money and to pay my rent. I spent my summer break catching up. By my fourth year, I was a few classes behind and far from my goal of graduating in 3.5 years. However, this is where fate tends to happen. A good friend I met after I pledged, helped me obtain a job at a local bank. The same bank that would help me build some relationships in real estate and educate me financially in regards to budgets, credit cards, business loans, real estate, and so on. The same bank where I met my first post college career boss that would offer me a job making $70k. The same bank that would fund my first real estate project with limited experience and purely off of relationships. So, shortcomings are what you make them. Was it a shortcoming or was it a shift?

No, I didn't graduate in 3.5 years. Who cares? And no, I didn't go to dental school, nor did I take over my uncle's practice. The goals I planned after high school weren't accomplished. So what did happen? I got a job at a bank that helped curate some relationships and shift my way of thinking that helped me discover my passion. I graduated from college with a bachelor's degree. I received a great job out of college from a client from the bank that rewarded me with friendships, relationships, my wife, and money that helped fund some of my new goals.

All of these series of events would not have been possible had I allowed myself to be judged by the world's definition of shortcomings and not my own. Had I not been willing to shift and instead viewed everything as a failure instead of a lesson. Had I not allowed myself to go with the new vision versus staying stuck in my old one. So remember, you are your own big system, and you can change as you see fit. No one controls you, but you.

Chapter Five: Time to Reflect

- ◊ Do you let society dictate your worth? If so, why and how can you change your mentality?

- ◊ Do you feel as though you are operating at your full potential? If not, what are some things that you can improve?

- ◊ Have you set 1, 3 and 5 year goals that are S.M.A.R.T (Specific, Measurable, Achieveable, Realistic, and Timely)? Write them down and check yourself on them quartely or bi-annualy to see your progression.

- ◊ Do you find yourself constantly comparing your success or accomplishments to those plans set by your parents or freinds? Maybe you have created goals that are S.M.A.R.T but you know that you are not truly putting in the hard work. How can you change your input to maximize your output?

- ◊ Reflecting on the last paragraph in this chapter, your life is YOUR LIFE! You have full control regardless of other people's plans, goals, words, etc. Live it on your terms and how you want to live. Be willing to accept the consequences or enjoy the rewards, either way you are in control!

Chapter Six

THE SHIFT

My life as a real estate developer can be synonymously compared to the game of golf. Every golfer, whether good or bad, knows that in the game you will experience bad shots that will make you want to break every club in your bag and walk off the course. But it takes that one time when everything aligns perfectly, your emotions are in sync, and you just let go of everything in your head. You step up to that tee, breathe in and out and...BOOM! The ball sails off the club, straight down the middle, and runs for a 305-yard tee shot! At that very moment, the other seventeen holes don't matter and you are already planning to return to the golf course next week. That's my life with real estate. My emotions are up and down. One month you're good, and the next month you're dealing with issues back-to-back. There is a constant wave of highs and lows, but by the end of the game there is a beautiful success story or a moment that sparks the will to continue. That spark then begins another chapter of stress, stretching, and growth! I am sharing my personal real estate journey with the hope that some readers understand that you don't have to have much to get started. Regardless, you will experience your share of peaks and valleys, but as long as you have the will and the drive to get started, and the consistency to stay at it, you will be successful.

My real estate journey began with inspiration from investors that I met while working at Simmons Bank in college. As most people are, I was somewhat motivated by money. I have come to learn the issue of being driven solely by money: Money isn't enough to sustain the vision. When entrepreneurs start their journey, they start with a vision to change the world, create a better process, or make things more functional for the people who will follow them. The vision is one of purity and selflessness. However, if money is the only motivator then it is easy to persuade that vision. Proverbs 17:16 says, "It is senseless to pay to educate a fool, since he has no heart for learning" (NLT Version). While at the bank I developed close relationships with my customers. I would even talk to some about their professional life as well as getting to know them on a personal level. There was one guy in particular who stood out to me as a Black professional and entrepreneur. During my time at the bank we had many one-on-one sessions where we would talk for thirty minutes at a time during slow periods. He really was a mentor to me and he never knew it. I would ask him about his many accounts and why different people would come and deposit money into them. I would ask him why he would have multiple transactions each time he came into the bank and moved money around. "What is it that you do man?" "Who are you and how did you become so successful?" Yes, I was that blunt. Partially because it was my job but mainly because I was curious. After he stopped staring at me, he dropped his head and began to chuckle. I sat there wondering if I went too far and if my questions were too direct. Instead, he looked up and said, "Young man, you are going to go far in life because you are not afraid to ask questions...and not only questions...THE QUESTIONS!" He went on by saying, "If more young people would only ask the questions they wanted real answers to, us elders would be more than happy to share our knowledge. But the answer to your question is, real estate."

Real Estate is what brought him opulence. Real estate is what brought him financial freedom. Real estate is what provided him with generational wealth. That was the key I needed. That was when I made up my mind. I no longer wanted to be a dentist, as a matter of fact my exact words were, "Fuck being a dentist, I don't want to stare in nobody's mouth no way!" It had nothing to do with the money because we know that being a dentist can reward you handsomely. It had more to do with what we talked about in Chapter 3—checking my passion. I thought I wanted to be a dentist to follow in my uncle's footsteps, but I didn't care about it as much as I thought. I knew immediately that my new plan was to finish up college with a degree in biology or health sciences and get a good job that would allow me to save for my future endeavors in real estate.

Back to the story: It was my senior year of college and I had just received my last refund check. I didn't need the extra $12,000, but I wasn't going to give it back to Uncle Sam either. So, I decided to put the money in my free, interest-bearing savings account. I was able to get one of those accounts as a perk for working at the bank. The semester goes by, and one day while I was at work, a gentleman entered. He was a real estate investor, owned a new pizzeria, and the manager at a new call center for Hewlett Packard that just opened earlier that year. We had been talking for several months now about life, real estate, school, and general business. I even signed him up for a business credit card with our bank at one point. Safe to say, he felt very comfortable talking to me and on that particular day offered me a job as soon as I finished college. Perfect! This was exactly what I needed as step one of my new plan.

Before we carry on, let's reflect for a moment on what I mentioned above about what it takes to get started. You need some money. Thanks to the refund disbursement, I could check that box. ***You don't need $12,000 to start!*** More importantly and even more than money in the beginning stages, is leveraging the connections you have. There is something you can learn wherever you are. Stay close to opportunities, seek curiosity, and fill yourself with knowledge. I didn't necessarily need $12,000, but it certainly didn't hurt. I was educated but not in the area of real estate, so I still needed that. However, my mentor offered me a great job and a chance to save some real money to prepare financially for my future real estate endeavors. Now, I was making some headway with the plans.

Fast forward to college graduation. I was a few months into my new job as an Enterprise Account Representative for Hewlett Packard. It was a Friday at work and a few of my coworkers, now longtime friends, decided to go out to a bar that night to celebrate the week. While I was sitting at the bar waiting for the others to show up, I started a conversation with a guy we'll call Tommy. During the small talk I asked Tommy what he did for a living? He told me that he was a full-time real estate investor. You can only imagine the level of excitement I felt. Once again, my future endeavor had presented itself. With a little excitement, I said, "Wow, I'm looking to get into that industry myself.

Any tips on how to get started?" Let's pause for a moment. What I just did is a great lesson to learn for any novice or professional investor. When wanting to get into any profession that you don't know about, be a sponge. Be prepared to listen for a long time and ask plenty of questions even if the information seems repetitive. People who are successful in their profession love to talk about what they do and definitely like to talk about their successes. Unfortunately, most successful people only talk about their wins, which you can get from anyone or any book. What you need to know is what that successful person did wrong. What were their losses? What pitfalls did they or should they have avoided? If they could do it all over again, what would they do differently? This is why people charge. If I can teach you how to avoid every mistake and land mine, this is what pushes you ahead faster, and that information comes with a price. However, if you can learn to listen—to what's said and not said—and ask questions, you can get the same game for free.

"The game is to be sold, not to be told." - Snoop Dogg

Sometimes people become diverted from their plans because they didn't have the money to pay for information that could've been given to them for free. Additionally, closed mouths don't get fed. You have not because you ask not. There has to be an intentionality and burning fire about the way you seek information that will propel you forward. Find mentors that are about that action. Go to the opposite side of the train tracks. Dream bigger. Take off your shackles.

On the flip side of the same coin, teachers must teach. To my beginners who are reading, one day you will have an overflow of information and resources. It will be your job to pass that on. To my experienced readers, consider a mentee. This eager learner could eventually become an ally or partner on future deals that benefit you both. This is generational healing. **To summarize, we are given two ears and one mouth so that we may listen twice as much as we speak. Teachers, this doesn't exempt the fact that we are to speak to those** ears that are willing to listen.

> *"Compliment the author and they will tell you how to write the story."*-RL Alexander

While still talking at the bar, Tommy told me he had a property that he was trying to get rid of and it'd be a perfect project to cut my teeth on. Without hesitation (and with all ignorance on the art of negotiation), I said I was in and asked him how much? He replied by asking how much I had? I told him $12,000 because that is what I had to spare thanks to my refund check from school. A few things to pay attention to. ***Try to avoid being the first to name a price.*** This is a common mistake made either out of anxiousness, nervousness, necessity to make the deal happen, or lack of knowledge. There is a saying in sales that when closing a deal, the first person to speak loses the deal. For instance, if you are closing a deal and you want $100,000 and the person asks you how much and you say, "$100,000," chances are, you open the door for negotiations, denial, and/or loss of money. It could also go perfect, and they pay you what you ask for. However, let's say they were prepared to pay more than $100,000, or $100,000 is a good price, but because you spoke first, now they see that number as a starting point and want to come down. My point? Begin by asking questions like: "What are you paying now?" "Do you have a price in mind that you were looking to pay?" "Have you received any other offers?" "What do you think this service is worth?" Open-ended questions like these allow the buyer to better understand the value of what you are offering. You must keep your poker face intact at all times. Foreplay. Coax a little. Don't get too jumpy too soon. The mistake I made was being very anxious and overly excited that I spoke first and gave him everything that I had.

Fast forward to closing on the property for $12,000 only to find out that my bar friend never owned the property but instead made a proxy deal to acquire the property only if he found a buyer. Today we call them wholesalers. These people act as a representative between the homeowner and agent, or buyer to make a cut on the deal depending on the sales price. This guy made $6,000 on the sale of a house he didn't even own. There is a business in this as well and we will talk about that later in the book. The property that I just closed on was a condemned property that had to be completely renovated and brought up to code. Condemned basically means that the property is slated for demolition unless the original owner decides to fix the property or sell it to a new owner who is willing to do the same. Having a condemned property as your first deal teaches you a lot about real estate. When working with a condemned property you are almost building a brand-new structure which means one would potentially go through each step of building a new home. This process allows the new investor to learn how to work with contractors, trades, city board members, inspectors, and even the bank when it comes to paying for different parts of the project. This was an instrumental part of my real estate development journey because no matter how many books I read or how many people I talked to, there was no level of textbook learning that would beat on-the-job training. For me and this particular project, I learned by making a lot of mistakes. *A failure makes the joy of success so much sweeter because you respect the feeling of going through a struggle only to come out victorious on the other side.*

Back to the project. My bar friend who became my teacher hooked me up with his construction crew out of Memphis, Tennessee. Not being prejudiced but from my personal observations and experience, in the South, real estate developers and investors mainly use Hispanics for construction projects. However, when picturing Memphis, Tennessee, one doesn't think of Hispanics, but of the Blues, barbeque, culture, and Black and white people. Naturally, I assumed his crew was going to be white males who had been working with him for years and knew exactly what he expected. NOPE! I was wrong. Let me introduce you to a few interesting characters here, because this is where it gets comical.

Introducing Pimp C: Pimp C's real name was Charles. I won't use his last name for anonymity, but he was a real pimp. Pimp C drove a 1999 Cadillac

Escalade that was painted a two-tone color—green and yellow like the Green Bay Packers. He always talked about the women he had that would do anything for him at the drop of a dime, no questions asked. But Pimp C, as the ladies called him, was able to take care of their issues because he knew everybody in Memphis and everyone owed him a favor or two. If they needed a light bill paid, help with gas money or a car payment, groceries, and in some cases free entry into the club, Pimp C was the plug. Don't play with Pimp C! He also had a construction license to build and rehab properties as long as it stayed under a certain limit. He definitely had the knowledge, skills, and experience and this is why he was the OG (Original Gangsta). Pimp C, being the don, had to have a crew of misfits right? A good crew of young gangstas (YGs) don't come without drama, and drama is necessary to tell a good story. So let's introduce the rest of the team.

Next up, Tiger! Tiger was about 4'10, weighed about 120 pounds, wet, and could fit in any space you needed him in. Tiger hated to be dirty, but would do what was necessary to get the job done. He also put you in the mindset of a spider monkey because of his ability to climb on things and get to certain places without all of the tools needed to accomplish the task. He didn't need a ladder or a stepping stool, Tiger was always competing for the Ghetto-lympics. Tiger had a problem though. He liked to shoot dice and gamble. The more people in the game, the better. He also loved big girls. When Drake shouted out "I like my women BBW," there was Tiger shouting, "Amen!" and "You too bro?!" The bigger, the better, and don't get me wrong, there's nothing wrong with big girls, they indeed need love too, but like I said, Tiger was 120 pounds. Wet.

Next up was Half Head. You either know him, or you don't. Half Head, who's real name I don't know, was the baddest roofer I had ever seen (even to this day). He was a one-man band. The work he did in a single day was the equivalent of three men, and he enjoyed every minute of it. There are vintage videos of NBA teams triple-teaming Michael Jordan, and him still doing some insane, incredible shit and getting a bucket. That was Half Head. Half Head got his name from a freak accident he incurred while working on a jobsite as a laborer in Memphis. One day while two or three stories in the air on steel beams of a building, Half Head wasn't properly harnessed or wearing his hard hat and fell to the ground. An accident that should have killed him left him with a severe brain injury, and after multiple surgeries, an inverted steel plate was placed in his skull that made him appear to have only half of a brain, or queue the nickname—Half Head. It's pretty messed up, but this is how these guys got along and communicated with each other.

Next, you have Popeye. He had his quirks too. Popeye was the carpenter who also liked to gamble, celebrated 4/20 every day, but always performed at work. He mainly liked structure. If you said we were starting at a particular time, then he'd start. If quitting time was at 5:00, at 4:45 Popeye was wrapping up the tools—leaving the site at 5:00 and not a second after. The funniest thing about Popeye and Tiger was that they would quit at least two times a week from something that pissed them off, and then by the end of the week they were happy again because it was payday. By Sunday, all their money was gone to Pimp C. It usually happened like this: Friday, after getting paid, they'd all go out to eat together. Saturday, they'd get a new sack, get high, and shoot dice. By Sunday, Pimp C had all their money. On Monday they'd need an advance on Friday's paycheck, which they'd get from Pimp C, who cyclically and ironically would end up with the money all over again. Insert definition of insanity here.

The last two people I want to introduce are Hustle Man and Blue. Legend is, Hustle Man was a true hustler. He slang that crack rock back in the '70s and at the time would have been what we know now to be a multi-millionaire. Hustle Man was full of knowledge, not just in construction, but in the streets too. For a Black man like myself, this is what gave me a leg up. Observing individuals like Hustle Man gave me a well-rounded education. Every day, I made sure to grasp and soak up whatever game was presented.

Now Blue, Blue was the right-hand man to Pimp C. Blue always rode in the front seat, was always the first to eat after Pimp C, and knew everything that was going on at any moment. If you couldn't get Pimp C, you called

Blue. Blue was a man of many skills, but organization was not one of them. His thoughts were just as scattered as his teeth. And I mean scattered. Blue probably had five teeth in his mouth. Total. Each one had a purpose. Blue loved chicken and bubble gum. One tooth was for chewing. One was for breaking down the food. And the three in the front were for grinning at the ladies who passed by. They usually didn't smile back, but Blue didn't really care. He swore he had game. He had teeth. Past tense. See, Blue had a drug problem at one point in his life that ruined the life he could've had. Like a cliche story, Blue grew up playing baseball and was pretty good, people say. Blue went to a predominantly white college, connected with the wrong people, wrong drugs, and took a hard downward spiral and became addicted to heroin and crack. Blue spent the majority of his thirties through late forties strung out on drugs, bouncing from job to job, and picking up whatever work he could. But let me tell you, Blue could lay carpet and have it tighter than your beautician's lace front. You couldn't even see the seams. He painted like nobody's business and laid tile straighter than Cardi who "got a bag and fixed my teeth." Pimp C found Blue in Memphis, took him in, gave him a place to stay, gave him work, and from there, their bond grew.

This group of guys gave me an opportunity to learn far more than the typical experience of simply hiring a contractor and paying them a fee. They taught me as I paid them—the good and the bad. They showed up for work—late. They made their problems my problems, which typically happens when you get comfortable, and they made me miss deadlines and fail inspections. They were notorious for cutting corners, getting hook-ups, and we'd constantly have to redo something. They got paid for services they didn't render well, and they almost burned down the house cooking food on a makeshift grill. However, what these guys did well far surpassed the things they did wrong. They were horrible cooks that made damn good cookies. The things they did wrong taught me valuable life, business, and financial lessons. I learned that friendships and business have a time and place and should not be intertwined. Friendships in business can make you vulnerable at times and more likely to excuse someone else's issues. For example, when the guys arrived late because they couldn't all get up in time to take a shower in a one bedroom and bath rent house, or when I missed an inspection because they didn't return to Little Rock from Memphis on Sunday night to be there Monday morning. Popeye ended up going to jail over the weekend and didn't get released until Monday. Valid reason to be late, but this wasn't my problem. I had to reach a deadline that couldn't be met because of the friendships I had created with my contract workers. I empathized with them and made it okay to give excuses. I traded professionalism for a huge savings on labor and sometimes material. I learned that "Everything that's free ain't good, and everything that's good ain't free." I gained street knowledge that made me stronger at negotiations and talking to people in the real estate game. I literally learned about carpentry, trades, and the steps to renovating a home from these guys. When they did complete a project, they went above and beyond and made sure that I was happy. When I needed them to come through and complete something due to a time constraint, they stayed later to make sure it was accomplished. Everything wasn't perfect, but the lessons learned were priceless.

Working on my first project that I purchased with my college refund check from a random guy at the bar, who in return lent me his Memphis crew was a challenge to begin with. For starters, I had very little knowledge on how to build a house. I didn't have a consistent mentor in the real estate flip game, therefore, ignorance hindered me from developing a fully calculated budget to bring the condemned home back to life. I didn't ask enough questions, and through my excitement I failed to stop and think about the things that were important to make me successful. I didn't have any connections with contractors or vendors other than my bank, therefore I set myself up to be taken advantage of. Similar to how car salesmen prey on the unknowledgeable, my ignorance could have cost me thousands. Walk in thinking you're going to get a $29 oil change, and leave with a $400 bill. Real estate is the same way for the illiterate.

"My people are destroyed for the lack of knowledge." -Hosea 4:6, KJV

I didn't have my exit strategies lined up for what I would do with the home after renovation, and overall I didn't properly prepare for the task that I was jumping into. However, I did do some things successfully. Although I didn't prepare a full budget for the renovation, I did devise financials to know exactly how much I would have to pay at the peak or end of the project. When all monies were drawn from the bank, I knew what my payment would be and was prepared to pay it. I had friends that were excited to see me dive into the project, one reason being that I was the guinea pig, the other reason out of pure excitement because they were able to witness a project of this magnitude.

Naturally, I am a salesman, so when I landed a contractor, I made a deal with him that enabled me to learn directly from the source as a part of the agreement. This connection led me to receiving hands-on experience for renovating a home. Let me reiterate what I just said. As a part of the deal I made, I put in bold print: Teach me everything you know. From there, he literally explained to me why we needed certain materials, why we had to put a beam or joist or 2x4 in a given area. "How do you complete an estimate?" "How do you complete a takeoff of material for a job?" "How do you frame a house and what does sixteen inches on center mean?" Some people might think that this is crazy and ask, "Why does he want to know all of that? Just hire professionals and get out of the way, right?" Wrong!! I needed to learn to speak the language so that no one would ever have the opportunity to take advantage of me. You see, the problem is, 80% of Americans don't ask enough questions about the services they're paying for. They simply look to see if they can afford the amenity and if it's in line with what other people are charging.

Peep what I'm saying in this scenario: Take two different news media outlets and you will get two different views. Two different opinions. Two different takes on one situation. Now let's loop in the consumer. Consumer A only watches Medio Outlet One and Consumer B only watches Media Outlet

Two. Consumer A swears their viewpoint is right because Media Outlet One backs their political views and says, "This is what happened," therefore, that's what happened, right? Consumer B, thinks their views are right because Media Outlet Two said, "No, Media Outlet One is wrong and this is what really happened and over here we only report the facts!" So, who holds the truth? In all honesty, in some cases, both of them, and many cases neither. The fact is, neither consumer will truly understand the full scope of a given story because they are only listening, regurgitating, and repeating what they heard from their chosen source. Both sides have an agenda and narrative to push and uphold, therefore, as a consumer we must be diligent in our own personal studies, not taking anything as absolute facts at face value. Being open to all sides and knowing the dangers in blindly trusting one source wholeheartedly allows us as consumers to reenter the world without stereotypes and prejudices against people, situations, and events that we have limited scope on. This is why it's essential to ask the right questions. This is why being inquisitive is important. The way knowledge is passed down is through teaching and learning. If we are only teaching and learning what we believe to be true and not other facts, viewpoints, and opinions, then that is what we call "biased-based learning and teaching."

The point I will continue to reiterate is this: Ask questions. Ask the same questions in different ways. Ask different people the same question and get different answers. For example, I asked two seasoned framers about using a laminated veneer lumber (LVL) beam over a single car garage versus two 2x12 beams that are sandwiched together with plywood in the center. One told me what he was taught and that LVL beams were stronger. The other framer told me that he was taught to use a LVL but realized that using two 2x12s with plywood sandwiched in between is the same thing yet stronger and cheaper as far as materials cost. Guess what? Both ways accomplished the same goal but because I was now informed and more knowledgeable, I could make a decision around going with the less expensive cost or going with the traditional method. The key is to come to a full understanding of the situation you are in before moving forward. The older generation inspired Mario Winans to sing "I don't want to know. If you're cheating, keep it on the low." This is not the way to be in real estate. Research, dig deep, and ask questions! By striking this deal with my contractor, I was able to pay him what he asked for and get educated also. This made the deal more lucrative for me.

One vital tool I learned to become successful in was politicking with city board members. I didn't say shucking and jiving, moreso learning the language of sales, communicating effectively, and occasionally going out for drinks. This is very important, as city board members have the power to stop your job right in the middle of its tracks.

Wanting to be one step ahead of myself, when the job was close to completion, I began searching for a renter. Sometimes the market is prime for selling, other times it is more profitable to rent. However, knowing and being able to follow such trends is vital, and because I did my fair share of research and asked the right questions, I was able to make the accurate decision at the time and rent. I asked my realtor for current market trends, which you should be able to attain from any legit realtor at any time when you are trying to decide whether selling or holding onto a property would be more beneficial. I asked, "Has there been any current sales in the area recently? How about rentals?" I asked, "What's your professional opinion around the target price for selling and renting?"

Buyers must also show inquisition. Buyers must know when it's the right time and in their advantage to purchase a home or else they can be caught holding an overpriced bag at the end of the deal. If you take a look at market trends in the state of Texas, for instance, they are usually in favor of the seller. This is due to supply versus demand. Because the population in Texas continues to grow at an exponential rate, there is a demand for more housing. This constant influx of newcomers is met with an unfulfilled demand—there are more people going to Texas than land to support the growth. Because of this, owners selling homes can demand a higher price point because the pickings are slim. On the flip side, take a state like California that has suffered from over-inflated housing prices and a mass exodus in population. Supply seems to be a nonfactor—buyers have their choice of housing and sellers have to be a little more creative and price conscious when selling their home. Take away moment: **Get as much professional advice as possible when thinking about buying or selling your home.**

Back to the story. I found a renter that paid on time for three months. By the fourth month, he came up with every excuse on why the house was not up to his standards and he shouldn't have to pay in full. "The house is too big." "The energy bill is too high." "There's no jacuzzi on the deck." "Can we paint the walls a new color?" I had to deal with evicting my first tenant, and had to create some cashflow or else watch my potential asset quickly turn into a liability. I placed the house up for sale only to have a terrible realtor with no action for three months which equated to a loss of income from having an empty house. The next step, out of desperation, was to put a family member in the home to help take some of the weight off the monthly payments I was responsible for. My family member stayed there several months, alleviating some of the money flow issues and allowing me to rethink my strategy and make a better decision. Five months later, I received a postcard from a local realtor who promised that he could sell my home for me in a very short amount of time.

 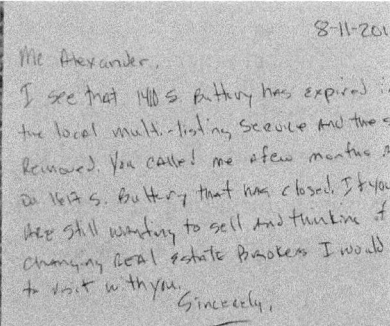

Let me clarify and say that this was the third postcard that I had received from him. I decided to give him a try only to find out that he was the guru of the neighborhood and knew all the facts about most homes in that area. He had been a realtor in the area where my property was located for the past twenty-five years and let it be known that he knew exactly what he was doing. Within two weeks, I received an offer at full asking price for the property. I couldn't have been more excited and apprehensive at the same time. Butterflies. I didn't want to get myself worked up for something that could potentially fall through. **However, there is power in positive thinking, and in this business, optimism is a standard.** The deal was successful, and after thrills, shrills, "Damns," and "Hallelujahs," we were able to close on my first property. But, I didn't want to be a one hit wonder, so the question loomed, "Now what do I do?"

In this business, you must educate yourself on the various tax laws. While you are learning, taking advice from a trusted CPA or tax lawyer will also prove to be beneficial. Never solely rely on the game given from an advisor, but let it be an add-on to the knowledge you are gaining from your personal studies. When searching for a good tax pro, there are a number of questions you should ask them to determine if they are good at their job or if they are a good fit for you. Ask questions like:

- What does your tax process look like?
- How can you help me with my tax goals?
- What can I do daily, weekly and monthly to improve my tax situation at the end of the year?
- Are you always available for me to call for tax advice or are you only accessible at the end of the year?
- What other services do you offer that can help me reach my goals?

It is crucial to find someone that you trust that aligns with your goals as a business and fits your personality. You will end up working very closely with this person if you are planning to build a strong business. The goal should be to never jeopardize your financial well-being.

To further educate myself, I went to real estate school to not only get my real estate license, but also to receive information from experts in the field. After two weeks of course work and studying, I scheduled to take my exam a week later. I passed on the first try! But here lies the question of, "Is it worth it?" As an agent, there are laws against being an investor and selling your own properties. There are laws that prevent you from representing yourself in your own transactions. Additionally, the required monthly licensing fees and the time spent to meet with clients and show houses didn't add up to the money I was making as the investor of the property. So I never activated my license which meant I never went to work for a realty company. This decision required the pros versus cons strategy where you weigh your options. And for me the choice was easy to make.

My next move was to reinvest my money and start my path to financial independence. One of my goals was to pay off the student loans my wife and I had acquired during our collegiate years. I took some of the funds I made from my first property to do just that, elevating my credit profile by lowering my debt to income ratio. After paying off our student loans, I invested in another property in order to continue the strategy of growing my real estate holdings portfolio.

My mom always told me that knowledge and education could take me anywhere. This proved to be a fact in my life, and I took what I gained and moved to Chicago for four years. While in Chicago, I teamed up with a friend I met after college and a local Chi-Town investor and purchased and flipped two properties. Having those early failures down South prepared me as I moved into this new market. As I negotiated equity splits and initial investments, I remembered the lessons I learned from Pimp C and Hustle Man. I remembered the early anxious mistakes I made with Tommy from the bar and remembering not to be the first one to speak. Every error, slip, and miscalculation that I made were lessons—lessons that I retained and later flipped to a success moment.

"Me, turn that 62 to 125, 125 to a 250. 250 to a half a million, ain't nothin' nobody can do with me, now who with me??"-Jay Z

Chapter Six: Time to Reflect

◊ When you choose to start something new, no matter if it is a sport, hobby, or career, change can be very daunting at times. One minute things are easy, comes naturally, no hard work is required, and this new venture feels like the greatest decision you ever made. Other times you are looking at yourself in the mirror wondering what the hell you have gotten yourself into. Either way, when the shift happens, how do you handle it?

◊ When you want to study your craft or see how far you can get, what are some of the questions that you ask to learn more? Are you direct in your approach or more lackadaisical?

◊ Life is a game of choices and consequences, both good and bad. Are you willing to play the game to become successful?

◊ Your network equals your net worth. How can you apply the principles learned from this chapter to your life and goals?

◊ Shift happens, but what will you do when you are in that situation?

Chapter Seven

EVERYONE CAN'T DRIVE THE BOAT

There's a saying that goes, "Everyone can't drive the boat!" Translation: You can't take everyone with you, and you definitely can't have them running your company for you. This statement may seem a little broad, so allow me to break it down. In the African American community, we tend to be our own worst enemy and critic. We judge and ridicule each other harder than we congratulate and build up one another. Though we aren't solely responsible for this harshness and what Dr. Carter G. Woodson considered "self-hate," we've established what many consider a crabs in a bucket mentality. On the contrary, we also have a tendency to try and bring our family and friends up as we climb the ladder. Many of us live by a code that we are our brother's keeper. That doesn't mean we have to be blood brothers or even a man, but we take responsibility for those closest to us. The problem with that is, we rarely make it to where we need to be before bringing up our family and friends. What tends to happen is, we carry more baggage up the hill, slowing down the process instead of making it up the hill and building steps along the way for our family and friends. Don't get me wrong, I'm big on family and ensuring that they are set up for success right along with me, however, in my experience, not everyone is needed right away, nor are they needed at the helm to help you steer the boat. Think about it like this: YOU put in the research, time, and patience with your process. YOU grinded when nobody had faith. YOU stepped out in the water. It would be silly of you, more than that, crippling of you to hand over the helm of your ship simply because somebody is your friend or related to you. Don't get me wrong, I'm not saying ALL family and friends make bad business partners, I'm simply stating not everyone is willing to risk their lives, their money, their time or energy in a vision that is not theirs. In business, it won't be hard to identify who you should include in your processes. Simply ask yourself this question: "Were they with me shooting in the gym?"

I've seen people want to get into real estate simply because they see the financial potential, but real estate can't just be about making money. You can and you will make great money in real estate but also in real estate you are changing people's lives. Families are buying your homes, putting a roof over their children's heads, cultivating futures, and creating their livelihood. If you are only thinking about making money, you will start cutting corners only to save a dollar, and you'll stop thinking about the lives you can affect with your selfishness and greed. The other part is, real estate is a risk. It's not like gambling at the casino where you feed a machine hoping that it hits, or you roll the dice hoping that you hit your number again in Craps. Real estate is a full time commitment and you have to be willing to commit yourself. Where there is risk, there is reward, and you better believe that the reward that comes from real estate is most definitely worth it. Real estate is a game of opportunity, demand, and sales. If the right opportunity presents itself, you have to take it and create a demand for your future product. People think that the sales part only comes when the realtor gets involved, but that couldn't be any further from the truth. The sales start immediately after you close the deal on the property and start working. **You have to sell yourself, sell your plan, sell your work, and sell the reason you are asking the price you are requesting for the property.** Before I got into real estate, I loved the game of Monopoly. I literally would play a single game for hours, even days with my cousins to determine a winner. I was hooked at an early age with the game, so you can imagine how thrilled I was to find out that I could play this game in real life.

Thanks to reality TV, real estate investing—whether buying and flipping, building, holding, or even inspecting—has become a trend that people are treating like a bandwagon to jump on. Before reality TV, people were not privy to the advantages of real estate investing outside of owning a home to live in. They were not familiar with the process of buying a secondary home, an investment property, and terms such as flipping, wholesaling, and holding. I love that the shows sparked interests and gave some education around real estate, because the industry was once foreign to many people, however, reality TV continues to microwave the real process and sweat equity. Essentially, this creates the illusion that it doesn't take skill or commitment to be in real estate when in fact, it does. Again, not everyone can drive the boat. A good captain knows how to delegate, has knowledge of the industry, a good team and proper preparation. If you are or have a good captain at the helm, the ship can go far, but you have to continually develop your skills and knowledge about the industry. Where is real estate going in the next few months, years, decades? Are there any initiatives that city governments or state governments are doing in the area you are investing in? Have you studied your craft to make sure you are ready? And I will continually stress the importance of a good team. As a leader, a project only goes as far as your vision. This means knowing how to delegate jobs and needs to the right people on your team. A good team can separate your business from failure and success. Having a good mentor on your team is necessary, and will elevate you as a leader.

Lastly, you have to be prepared. The word opportunity is defined as a set of circumstances that makes it possible to do something. Conquered opportunities become golden. People will see your successes as luck. But, you? You know better. You fell in love with the grind. Land ain't free and knowledge costs time, so earn your way through the process, educate yourself, and live in knowing that faith without work is sho' nuff dead. It's only hard work that breeds success!

"They gon love me for my ambition. Easy to dream a dream, though it's harder to live it." -Wale

"I seen it, I thought it, I dreamed it. I said it, I did it, I meant it. I taste it, I loved it, I need it. I want it, more of it, I fiend it." -Nipsey Hussle

Chapter Seven: Time to Reflect

- ◊ Do you have family and/or freinds that expect to ride along with you for the hardwork you have put in? They expect to be center court even though they never helped you practice or prepare for the game? How do you handle these situations?

- ◊ How do we change the naritive that we have a "crab-like" mentality or that it is a dog eat dog world that we are living in? I know one person can't change the world's view, but how can you change your personal one? What can you do differently to help bring your brother/sister up with you versus feeling like you are carrying them?

- ◊ Do you believe in yourself enough to grind hard when no one is pushing you, congratulating you, watching you? Do you need attention in order to be successful?

- ◊ Are you preparing yourself for the opportunity before it arrives? Some people say they would be different if they were given an opportunity (and that may be true) but are you prepared when the opportunity presents itself?

- ◊ Nothing comes to a sleeper but a dream, but in your reality you can make that dream come true!

Chapter Eight

THE MISSING PIECES OF THE PUZZLE

Imagine you are working on a 500 piece complex puzzle. You have been working on it tirelessly—day and night—taking breaks when you can, getting help when necessary, and when you finally start to see the light at the end of the tunnel you realize that there are several pieces of the puzzle missing. You can't finish a puzzle that has missing pieces. Hell, how can you even figure out the rest of it if you don't know which pieces are missing? This analogy explains how I felt going through my beginning years in real estate. There is only so much studying you can do. There are only so many questions you can ask. However, the biggest obstacle I faced when I did my studying and when I asked my questions is that I would only get half of the information. It seemed as if some of the information was withheld on purpose. It almost felt like a right of passage that I had to go through so much just to piece the information together.

In an earlier chapter I talked about Greek Life in college and when I pledged Kappa Alpha Psi. Before joining the organization I conducted my research on what their principles were and why they were formed. I took into account the time period, racial tension, social status, and the aim of upward mobility these young men envisioned when they came together to create a bond that exists over 110 years later. I then asked myself why I wanted to join that particular organization. Whatever conclusion I came to, I still had to be accepted by the members who were already a part of the organization. They had to learn about me and decide if I was the right fit for their organization. This process to get to know me came through pledging, and pledging on the former end consisted of tasks-oriented projects, questions, one-on-ones, labor and in some cases, homework. This is, of course, the clean version. There was definitely more to it, but for the sake of this example, we will let the grey areas be. The process of what my prophytes were doing was seeing how I integrated into their system and how I could continue the legacy which was created in 1911. However, until I was fully indoctrinated, they purposely withheld knowledge about the organization so that I would not have all the information needed to go do something else with another organization. They purposely withheld pieces of the puzzle until they deemed me fit to be a part of their organization. These same tactics have been used by the wealthy to keep information from the lower and middle classes. Many times information is withheld purposefully. Sometimes it's simply because we haven't had the proper exposure points that will even allow us to think down a certain path. It may seem unfair, but just like I wanted to join my fraternity, I had to prove myself worthy, in a sense, to gain access. I personally feel that is the same for joining the elite or the one percent. I have to continually prove—through my dedication, research, and innovation to the industry—my worth, in order to gain access to the purposely withheld missing pieces.

What if we gave everyone all the information and all the answers without working for it? How would we treat that privilege? If history has taught us anything, it has taught us that anything given without work is mistreated, unappreciated, and squandered. Look at unemployment in some cases. Look at government assistance in some cases. Don't get me wrong, all of these are not wholly bad and some people use them correctly, but many don't. If all of the information was given away, would there still be a huge disparity between the poor, low income, middle class, high class, and the wealthy? My best guess is, probably. Not due to any supremacy, but simply because of mindset shifting. On one hand, by the time the masses are given information, there is already a new culture being trickled down by the elite. On the other hand, there is nothing new under the sun, and although language may shift, trends and fads tend to recycle themselves.

Therefore, for those of us who are willing to grind and put in the work, we have to be willing to acknowledge that there are missing pieces due to injustices, miseducation, illiteracy, and an overall lack of resources. After this acceptance, we must choose to thug it out. No, you weren't born with a silver spoon. No, the missing pieces may not be in your neighborhood or immediate social circle. No, these aren't reasons to hang your head and give up in pity, but instead, commit to finding those missing puzzle pieces. Commit to setting your family free. Commit to setting yourself free. Commit to the work. It will be so worth it.

Chapter Eight: Time to Reflect

◊ Do you understand that you will not have all the answers? Furthermore, all the answers will not be given to you but are you willing to get off your ass and go find them? What steps can you take today to assist you in getting the help or the answers you need?

◊ What does the word privileged mean to you? Do you think you have privilege or do you lack it? How does it affect your thinking process either way?

◊ Understand that nothing worth having comes easy or free. However, there is a liberating feeling knowing that you put in the hardwork, regardless of the privilege or lack thereof. Reflect on your problems, think about your excuses, and then throw it all out while focusing on the solution.

◊ There is and will always be a missing piece to the puzzle!

Chapter Nine

THE UNCOMMON MILLIONAIRE

In 2016 I had the opportunity to meet a prominent, sought-after speaker and President of Game Time Budgeting, a Cincinnati-based financial education firm that provides dynamic and engaging financial wellness programs for employees, financial literacy workshops for students, and virtual coaching. Alfred D. Riddick Jr., who goes by Al Riddick, spoke to a room of one hundred people including myself on the importance of money management and financial literacy. He has authored several books and has personally signed *The Uncommon Millionaire* for me. In *The Uncommon Millionaire*, Al discussed principles that he and his wife applied in order to get out of debt that involved student loans, mortgages, credit cards, and spontaneous spending. I bring up this book because it spoke to me in ways that enriched my caliber of thinking. "Financial success begins with behavior!"

This message can also be related back to real estate: financial success begins with behavior. *We must condition our minds and behaviors to operate in a manner in which we have already made it to the position of power that our goals were set on in the beginning.* When I made up my mind that I wanted to start investing in real estate I created a plan to start paying off my debt, saving thirty percent or more of my paychecks, creating side hustles that would lead to extra income and extra savings, and making sure that my credit was top-notch. I did these things because I knew that at the very least these would be the items that could derail my plans of becoming successful. Be on the forefront of eliminating any and all reasons the bank could possibly say "No" to your million dollar plan. As the captain, the writer, the CEO, it is on you to have your shit together!

Chapter Ten

GET YOUR SHIT TOGETHER

If you have managed to make it this far in the book and still wonder, "What can I be doing to better prepare myself for investing in real estate?" Below are my answers to that question. Note, these points aren't just for real estate but can be applied to most goals or investment plans that you set for yourself. Let's get into my top five recommendations.

    1. **Recognize where you are and where you need to be.** In the back of this book I will attach a PFS or Personal Financial Statement Worksheet. The PFS will help you assess all of your current income and liabilities. This worksheet will require that you include every piece of debt that you have from personal credit cards to student loans, from auto loans to mortgages, and even the money that you owe Reggie that you didn't pay back after he bought you lunch at work. Okay, so it might not include the last part, but the point is you need to include everything and be completely honest with yourself as this is a snapshot of your current situation. By recognizing where we are, we can now develop a plan of where we need to be. By understanding our PFS snapshot we can create a roadmap of achieving debt relief, thus begin to better understand financial literacy and develop a strategy to invest in whatever capacity we see fit.

    2. **Find the money gremlin.** In the movie, Gremlins, there were these little ugly creatures that were a terror to everyone. They multiplied by water, ate any and everything, destroyed households, and pillaged whatever was in their tracks. It is on us to find the money gremlin in our lives. Many of us have terrible spending habits. We tend to think that as long as the money is in the account and our bills are paid then it's okay to spend as we want. However, what happens is, we swipe that debit card without tracking it, and before we know it, we're looking at an empty account. Flat broke. The first thing we think about is, "Where did all my money go?" We'd like to believe that there are some

little ugly, magical gremlins out there stealing our money, when in fact we are not properly monitoring our account. Take charge. You are the master of your own fate. Don't be the gremlin in your own life that causes you to continually fall back in your goals due to immaturity and overspending. This is all a part of financial literacy and understanding our financial journey.

3. **What is your six month to one year plan?** Goal setting is a lost art that needs to be retaught and reestablished. What's the importance of goal setting? Imagine preparing to take a trip and you're driving to your destination. You don't know where you are going and how long it will take to get there. The GPS is useless because you don't have a set landmark. So the question remains the same, what is your six months to one year plan? Where are you going? Once you have a destination, you can now open up the GPS in order to identify the proper route to take. How should you be budgeting based on your plans? Set goals that are considered S.M.A.R.T: Specific, Measurable, Achievable, Relevant, and Timely. When I started out in my real estate investing career I would use this template to set goals for myself to move one step closer to the next phase. Notice, I didn't say the finish line, but the next phase. When I set my goals I never want it to look as a point of completion, but instead a point of observation and reflection. Always allow your goals to continue to grow and set checkpoints to observe, reflect, and reset.

4. **Educate yourself.** LEARN! LEARN! LEARN! Cliche statement: Education is key when it comes to being successful. We have to be and remain sponges, soaking up the knowledge that we read in books, get from sponsors, mentors, and learn from the mistakes and successes of others. I can't tell you how much time I put into learning and perfecting my skills in real estate. One thing that I would do when I began to educate myself was finding ways to immediately apply the knowledge I had just learned. Whether it was having a debatable conversation, speaking with one of my mentors and asking them clarification questions, applying the information on the job, or even writing down what I heard or saw for retention, I found these practices to be the best and most effective ways for me to retain new and growing information.

5. **Push through adversity and setbacks.** You are resilient and you have to know that. Continually walk in tenacity knowing that nothing and nobody can separate you from your dreams… except giving up. So don't give up. Sounds simple because it is. Easy, no, but who asked for easy? I tell this story to all of my mentees that ask about getting into real estate and even those who are already successful but love to share stories: Since 2012 when I first started in

real estate, I have never had a project go smoothly. In every project, I've been robbed, materials have been broken, and I've paid for something twice more than a few times. In golf we say PAR for the course, which also means, it's expected. Real estate is not all glamorous, at least not on the investor's side of the business. However, the main point is, no matter what the adversity or set of circumstances are, push through if you want to be successful. It is okay to cry in the moment and it is okay to take a step back in the face of adversity, but it is never okay to lay down and quit… unless you want to be a quitter! I have taken my licks and I continue to take my punches, but I know that it is a part of the game. If I want to one day say I am a successful billionaire, I know this will only be accomplished by going through the mud and getting through those challenging times.

Chapter Ten: Time to Reflect

- **Action Item:** Find you a Personal Financial Statement to fill out and complete it immediately. Regardless of what you are doing or planning to do, it is important to know where you are. Be prepared. Most loan officers at banks have these forms in pdf format or you can Google a downloadable edition.

- **Action Item:** Create your financial plan. Find the money gremlin, where is your debt going? Did you create a short and long term financial goal?

- Education is key! Be a sponge and learn from whoever, whenever.

- Adversity is apart of life. Once you can accept that then nothing should come as a shock. You must practice resilience, learn to expect the setback and push your way through them.

Chapter Eleven

MAKE YOUR NEXT MOVE YOUR BEST MOVE

Que in the outro! Play that Boyz II Men! We're at the end of our first journey together. You've read some of my experiences and what I have gone through by now, therefore you should know and find assurance that your own experiences, fears, doubts, and uncertainties are not uncommon. However, what is consistent or common is the result of not starting or taking that chance. We are all educated in some form or another, whether it is book knowledge, street knowledge, or a cross fade of them both. It can be personal experiences that teach us, or the experiences of others. Wisdom comes from all, but how you use it depends on YOU.

In this book I have provided some of the fundamental steps and principles that can help get you started. So what's next? Make your next move your best move! How many times have we heard this saying and possibly used it for the wrong reasons? This time I am challenging myself and you to make your next step a step in the right direction, in a forward direction that is going to get you that much closer to your goal. I primarily talk about real estate investing in this book and my journey but the lessons can be applied to whatever your passion or dream is. In Chapter 9, I reference Al Riddick's book, *The Uncommon Millionaire,* because the name alone stands out. Why is it uncommon for someone to be a millionaire? Not in the simplistic sense of less than ten percent of the population are millionaires, but why is the process of becoming a millionaire uncommon? It's because we tend to forsake the simplistic principles that it takes to become a millionaire. Cutting costs, living below our means, saving more money than we spend, paying off debt, making wise investments with good to high returns, **building your network to increase your net worth**, investing in real estate and so on. These are all very smart decisions to make and apply that open doors to become a millionaire. It's not new math, nor groundbreaking strategies, and it is not anything new that other millionaires haven't done. It's all about application and consistency and that is what makes it uncommon!

So how does my future life look? I wake up one random morning and realize that it's Friday. My wife is awake making breakfast for the kids as they prepare for school. The kids have all that they need and are not wanting for anything. My wife is a stay-at-home mom who practically runs the household, the family organization, is involved with the Parent-Teacher Association (PTA) at the kids' schools, and also makes sure that I have my shit together. I am a self-employed real estate developer, along with other business ventures that have finally started to make seven figures annually, and in that moment I realize that this is the dream I had early on in my life. This is why I worked hard day and night, missed some of my kids' events, came home late, not talking to my family; not because I was angry but because I was tired from talking to clients all day. This is why I sacrificed sleep. I had a lifestyle that I planned would bring me peace, joy, and happiness. These are the things I hoped money could buy. But does the end justify the means? I sure hope so. And maybe the smiles on my family's faces provide proof. However, before I get to this day I must remember why I am doing this and who I am doing it for and everything will work out the way God intended it to.

Chapter Eleven: Time to Reflect

- **Action Item:** Do the work! Don't read this book once and put it out of reach. It was written to be a quick read to help you refelct on my past, my beginings and for you to see that we are not any different. Apply yourself at all times and do the work.

- If you don't want to read the book again, look at the "Time to Reflect" at the end of each chapter and refocus. Shift happens but its how you overcome the setbacks that help write your story.

- **Action Item**: READ THE BOOK when worry, stress, anxiety, etc sets in.

- **Action Item**: Create your financial plan. Find the money gremlin, where is your money going? Did you create a short and long term financial goal?

SYNOPSIS

So what's next? You have read the book, you have taken the classes, and you have watched the DIY and HGTV shows. But what is next? How do I follow up? How do I take that next step forward? My encouragement is for you to do the very thing that you have been scared to do~get your feet wet and dive into your first deal. You are not expected to get it right the first time. A good friend of mine, who is also my golf instructor, told me that, "when you first start trying new swings or learning different movements with the club, it is one hundred percent his expectation for me to fail!" After laughing he would go on to say, "Because from here we can only get better." This same principle needs to be applied when getting started in real estate or whatever it is that has been gnawing at you to try. You must expect that you won't get everything right on your first go, maybe not even your second time, but you will learn and avoid making the same mistakes in the future. After you read this book, it is my ask that you keep it close. Keep it close enough to pick back up and read where I have failed and overcome. Pick it back up and read when you feel discouraged about the wall that you keep hitting. For those who are trying to gain financing from the bank, pick it back up when they keep telling you, NO or that you don't have everything they are looking for. These are all just roadblocks that you are not the only one experiencing but its how you overcome these roadblocks that help create your story of triumph and success. Don't let this book be a one and done read. However, if you find yourself needing more one on one attention or understanding reach out to me at www.rlalexander.com and book some consultation time.

APPENDIX

In this section I will add a few documents and worksheets that I use in order help myself stay prepared for the banks and other financial partnerships. It is important to have your life and financial matters in order before jumping into any business or hustle. The following forms have helped me and I am sure can help you.

Below is a copy of a personal financial statement that I used when applying for commercial loans. Completing this form provides a snapshot of your financials and can help set the foundation for your goals. My advice is to update this form every six months to a year in order to document your journey on becoming finanlly successful.

First Service Bank

FINANCIAL STATEMENT
PERSONAL

(BOTH SIDES OF THIS STATEMENT MUST BE COMPLETE)

SCHEDULE A — CASH - DEPOSITORY RELATIONSHIPS

TYPE ACCOUNT	ACCOUNT IN NAME OF	WHERE DEPOSITED	AMOUNT

SCHEDULE B — LIFE INSURANCE - FACE VALUE & CASH VALUE

FACE VALUE	NAME OF COMPANY	BENEFICIARY	CASH VALUE	LOANS

SCHEDULE C — LISTED SECURITIES - ACTIVELY TRADED

NUMBER OF SHARES	MARKET VALUE EACH	MARKET VALUE TOTAL	DESCRIPTION OF SECURITIES	IN NAME OF

SCHEDULE D — UNLISTED SECURITIES - NOT ACTIVELY TRADED - Closely Held

NUMBER OF SHARES	BOOK VALUE EACH	BOOK VALUE TOTAL	TOTAL SHARES OUTSTANDING	DESCRIPTION OF SECURITIES

SCHEDULE E — REAL ESTATE OWNED

LOCATION OF PROPERTY	TITLE IN NAME OF	DATE ACQUIRED	COST	MARKET VALUE	PAYMENT AMOUNT	MORTGAGE BALANCE	MATURITY

SCHEDULE F — PARTIAL INTEREST IN REAL ESTATE OWNED

LOCATION OF PROPERTY	TITLE IN NAME OF	DATE PURCHASED	ORIGINAL COST	MARKET VALUE TODAY	MORTGAGE OWING	EQUITY VALUE	PERCENT OWNERSHIP

SCHEDULE G — ACCOUNTS & NOTES RECEIVABLE

PAYMENTS DUE FROM	ORIGINAL BALANCE	CURRENT BALANCE	FREQUENCY OF PAYMENTS	PAYMENT AMOUNT	COLLATERAL

SCHEDULE H — DEBT DUE BANKS, FINANCE COMPANIES & OTHERS

NAME OF LENDER	ORIGINAL BALANCE	CURRENT BALANCE	FREQUENCY OF PAYMENTS	PAYMENT AMOUNT	MATURITY DATE	COLLATERAL

My cousin, who is an attorney, created a workbook (initially for our family) titled "My Legacy Planning Portfolio". The purpose of this workbook is to provide a workspace for family members to document key information in one space and organize the things that family members will need to know at the time of your death. Although a lot of us hate to think about death, as you build and grow your assets with the hopes of leaving a legacy for your family you must prepare and have your life's documents in one place that your spouse, children, or family can get to. I won't talk much about the whole book, but I did pull out a few sections that I think are highly relevant to my book and pasted them in the pages to follow.

"We sometimes live robust and/or complicated lives. However, our family members may not know the full extent of our assets. You want to give them a road map to your life." - Chantel Mullen, Esq.

Storage Unit	
Address	
Contents Description	
Access – how to access and who is authorized	
Address	
Contents Description	
Access – how to access and who is authorized	

Safe Deposit Box	
Financial Institution	
Address	

Real Property	
Address	
Percentage of ownership	
Co-owners	
Contact Info	
Description	

Personal Property and Special Items			
Description		Location	
Description		Location	
Description		Location	
Description		Location	
Description		Location	
Description		Location	
Description		Location	
Description		Location	
Description		Location	

Most people have some form of bank account, bank card, Cash App, Pre-paid Debit card, etc. And in many cases their family members don't know about it (because they didn't want them to know so they wouldn't ask for money) because they just didn't mention it. Some people have accounts that they only use for saving money and they don't get a debit card or check book on that account. What do you think happens when they die and didn't tell anybody about the money, where it is or how to get access to it? The government keeps it and it happens more times than you think. The cliché statement I hear all the time is that, "You can't take it with you!" By using the workbook that Chantel Mullen, Esq has created, you can be at peace knowing that your family is taken care of and has taken care of you.

"People often have bank accounts, IRAs, stocks, bonds, and other investments, and neglect to tell family members about them." -Chantel Mullen, Esq.

Account Type	___ Savings ___ IRA/Keogh Account ___ Checking ___ Money Market ___ Stock ___ Certificate of Deposit
Institution Name	
Account Number	
Account Holder	
Account Co-holder	
State account opened in	

Account Type	___ Savings ___ IRA/Keogh Account ___ Checking ___ Money Market ___ Stock ___ Certificate of Deposit
Institution Name	
Account Number	
Account Holder	
Account Co-holder	
State account opened in	

Account Type	___ Savings ___ IRA/Keogh Account ___ Checking ___ Money Market ___ Stock ___ Certificate of Deposit
Institution Name	
Account Number	
Account Holder	
Account Co-holder	
State account opened in	

Account Type	___ Savings ___ IRA/Keogh Account
	___ Checking ___ Money Market
	___ Stock ___ Certificate of Deposit
Institution Name	
Account Number	
Account Holder	
Account Co-holder	
State account opened in	

Other Financial Accounts

There are accounts that your family will need to know because they may need make payments or close out accounts following your death. List those accounts here.

Retirement Accounts	___ 401K ___ Pension Plan ___ Deferred Compensation
	___ IRA ___ Keogh Plan
	___ Roth IRA ___ Social Security ___ Other: _____
Institution Name	
User Name	
Login/Password	
Website	
Account Contact	

Retirement Accounts	___ 401K ___ Pension Plan ___ Deferred Compensation
	___ IRA ___ Keogh Plan
	___ Roth IRA ___ Social Security ___ Other: _____
Institution Name	
User Name	
Login/Password	
Website	
Account Contact	

Investments	___ *Brokerage* ___ *Annuities* ___ *Line of Credit* ___ *US Savings Bonds* ___ *Bonds* ___ *Mutual Funds*		
Institution Name			
Account Number			
Website			
User Name		Password	
Account Holder		Account Co-holder	

Investments	___ *Brokerage* ___ *Annuities* ___ *Line of Credit* ___ *US Savings Bonds* ___ *Bonds* ___ *Mutual Funds*		
Institution Name			
Account Number			
Website			
User Name		Password	
Account Holder		Account Co-holder	

Residence	___ *Mortgage* ___ *Home Equity* ___ *Line of Credit*		
Institution Name			
Account Number			
Account Holder			
Account Co-holder			
Description of Property			
Website			
User Name		Password	

Residence	___ *Mortgage* ___ *Home Equity* ___ *Line of Credit*
Institution Name	
Account Number	
Account Holder	
Account Co-holder	

Description of Property			
Website			
User Name		Password	

Student Loan			
Account Holder			
Account Number			
Website			
User Name		Password	

Student Loan			
Account Holder			
Account Number			
Website			
User Name		Password	

Credit Card			
Account Holder		Co-Account Holder	
Account Number			
Card Name		Website	
User Name		Password	

Credit Card			
Account Holder		Co-Account Holder	
Account Number			
Card Name		Website	
User Name		Password	

Credit Card			
Account Holder		Co-Account Holder	

Account Number			
Card Name		Website	
User Name		Password	

Vehicle Loan			
Account Holder		Co-Holder	
Account Number			
Creditor		Website	
User Name		Password	

Vehicle Loan			
Account Holder		Co-Holder	
Account Number			
Creditor		Website	
User Name		Password	

Other Debt			
Account Holder		Co-Holder	
Account Number		When is payment due	
Creditor		Website	
User Name		Password	

Other Debt			
Account Holder		Co-Holder	
Account Number		When is payment due	
Creditor		Website	
User Name		Password	

Other Debt			
Account Holder		Co-Holder	

Account Number		When is payment due	
Creditor		Website	
User Name		Password	

Other Debt			
Account Holder		Co-Holder	
Account Number		When is payment due	
Creditor		Website	
User Name		Password	

Historical Information (For Obituary)

Your Full Name			
Date of Birth			
Birthplace			
US Citizen	☐ Yes ☐ No	Date naturalized	
Spouse/Partner		Dates of Marriage	
Spouse/Partner		Dates of Marriage	
Spouse/Partner		Dates of Marriage	
Name of Parent			
Birthplace of Parent			
Name of Parent			
Birthplace of Parent			
Your Occupation			

Notes

Notes

Notes

www.ingramcontent.com/pod-product-compliance
Lightning Source LLC
LaVergne TN
LVHW020937090426
835512LV00020B/3403